LITTLE BOOK OF
ADULTING

Quentin Parker

summersdale

THE LITTLE BOOK OF ADULTING

Copyright © Summersdale Publishers Ltd, 2018

Text by Abi McMahon

All rights reserved.

No part of this book may be reproduced by any means, nor transmitted, nor translated into a machine language, without the written permission of the publishers.

Condition of Sale
This book is sold subject to the condition that it shall not, by way of trade or otherwise, be lent, resold, hired out or otherwise circulated in any form of binding or cover other than that in which it is published and without a similar condition including this condition being imposed on the subsequent purchaser.

An Hachette UK Company
www.hachette.co.uk

Summersdale Publishers Ltd
Part of Octopus Publishing Group Limited
Carmelite House
50 Victoria Embankment
LONDON
EC4Y 0DZ
UK

www.summersdale.com

Printed and bound in Malta

ISBN: 978-1-78685-523-7

Substantial discounts on bulk quantities of Summersdale books are available to corporations, professional associations and other organisations. For details contact general enquiries: telephone: +44 (0) 1243 771107 or email: enquiries@summersdale.com.

Contents

Introduction

Adulting is the subtle art of always knowing what you're doing (or the even subtler art of pretending that you know what you're doing). It is about being better than basic, a step above the bare minimum, where you are required to master the balance between responsibility and having fun.

An adult eats three meals a day without getting food poisoning. Someone who's adulting cooks delicious, nutritious meals served on matching crockery.

An adult has a drawer that contains their important paperwork. Someone who's adulting stores their paperwork in binders.

An adult doesn't leave piles of washing-up next to the sink. Someone who's adulting can unblock the sink. Oh yeah – we're talking self-sufficiency, baby.

So you'd like to learn the ancient art of adulting? Turn the page and begin.

? 🤔

MIND

Time management

Do you feel as though you're constantly running out of time, while other 'perfect' adults seem to be able to make three-course meals, work overtime, clean the house to a shine and squeeze in a cheeky 5-mile run? Trust us, you're the normal one. Most adults feel as though there simply isn't enough time to do everything. But there are ways you can help yourself out...

WHAT ARE YOU REALLY UP TO?

For one week, sit down at the end of every day with the chart overleaf and write down what you've done and how long it took. Then add up the duration of each activity to work out your total time spent doing each of them. For example, how many hours a week do you spend cooking, how many vegging out in front of a screen and how many on chores?

	Monday	Tuesday	Wednesday	Thursday	Friday	Saturday	Sunday	Total
Food prep and cooking								
Ablutions, including beauty routine								
Commuting								
Work								
Chores								
Exercise								
Leisure (relaxation)								
Leisure (hobbies)								
Sleep								
Other								

AND WHAT DO YOU REALLY CARE ABOUT?

Once you've totted up your hours, grab a fresh sheet of paper and make two new lists. The first should feature areas you'd like to improve upon. Do you feel like you don't get to see your friends enough? Are you struggling to stay on top of the housework? Now make a second list comprising the most important things in your life. What makes your heart sing and your sun rise?

OK, it's comparison time! Take a peek at all the totals and see how they stack up against your two lists. Consider reducing anything that is taking up a lot of your time but doesn't feature highly on either list. Take a hard look at the things you've rated as most important to you and if you're not putting a lot of time into them ask yourself why. Adults do all the necessary things (don't even think about using this task as an excuse to quit work and spend all day playing video games) but they also put their hard-earned time into doing things that they love.

PRACTICAL MAGIC

Here's a little juju to help you transfer your plans from paper to real life.

No means no

Trust your gut. If you're beset with dread as soon as your colleagues mention after-work drinks, say no. If you really don't have time to whip up a cake for a bake sale, say no. An important stage of adult puberty is exchanging that faint whiff of guilt that allows you to be suckered into all sorts of unwelcome events for a deep aroma of self-knowing that allows you to live your life as you intended.

Cut it out!

Now you've started saying no to all those unwanted activities it's time to clean up after Past You's mistakes. Quit the netball practice that's making you miserable, set time limits on the video game that's eating into romantic time with your partner and finally work up the courage to hand in your notice as social secretary of your work's lunch club. Then use that sweet free time to enjoy the things you really love.

Delegate

It's a truth universally acknowledged that some people in shared housing do fewer chores than they should.

However, if you're really spending hours on end scrubbing the bath and lugging the rubbish to and fro, delegate. Instigate a chore chart, assign specific responsibilities or maybe offer little rewards for tasks achieved (even adults respond well to gold stars).

Wake up!

It's a beautiful morning! A lie-in, like a message from a distant friend, is all the sweeter for its rarity. So save it. Plus, you'd be amazed at what you can do with a few extra hours at the weekend. You could rustle through all the tidying or sweat through a 30-minute workout before breakfast. Whammo! You then have the whole day to enjoy yourself, free of anxiety about what you should be doing.

WHAT'S YOUR TIME HOROSCOPE?

Read the time profiles below and tag yourself according to which one suits your personality most, then follow the arrow to your horoscope.

Procrastinatus

Sensitive, friendly to all, gets overwhelmed when tackling big tasks.

Schedulesces

Curious, loves trying new things.
Plans easily slip their mind.

Union

Fun-loving, seizes the moment. A tendency for too much play and not enough work.

This is the week to prevent big tasks building up. Tag little chores onto the end of everyday actions, like washing-up when you take your plates to the sink or tidying a few bits when you get up to go to the loo.

With an organisational waxing moon, seize the opportunity to make lists. Write a list every morning of what needs to be done that day and tick off things when you complete them. Keep the list to hand so you can jot down new tasks as they come to mind.

With messy Mercury in retrograde, it's the moment to face up to the hard stuff. Block off one or two hours a week as 'blitz hours' and work your way through your important but un-fun tasks.

There are a lot of pressures when you're adulting so it's important to take care of yourself. Being successful is about health and happiness rather than trying to squeeze as much as possible out of your day. If you're feeling the crunch, try some of these techniques.

HEALTHY BODY, HEALTHY MIND

Your mind is a super-powerful computer and just like a computer it needs the right amount of power to run. A good diet, exercise and plenty of sleep are the foundations of a healthy mind. You are both your own admin assistant and boss. It's not just a matter of going to the doctor's when you're feeling poorly, you also have to maintain your health with other appointments. Schedule in time for the dentist twice a year and an optician every two years. If you're feeling under pressure, see if you can make any lifestyle changes. Sugar provides a lot of energy but our bodies burn through it quickly, providing a 'high' that is followed by a 'low'. Swap the sugary snacks for bites that are rich in useful vitamins and minerals, such as pumpkin seeds, unsalted peanuts and edamame beans, which are high in zinc, a natural anti-depressant. Try to hit those five-a-day targets too – you'll feel better for it!

MEDITATION

Meditation is a great habit to get into. It provides a welcome moment of respite for busy and overworked minds. Here's an easy 10-minute meditation technique for beginners:

- Find a quiet spot and sit.

- Close your eyes and relax.

- Focus on your surroundings, the noises you can hear and the sensations you can feel.

- Don't worry if thoughts come to mind, but try not to dwell on them and return your focus to your body when possible.

- Breathe in and out slowly, concentrating on the feeling of taking in and releasing the air. Repeat ten times.

- Try to incorporate this into your daily routine to give your mental health a helping hand.

MINDFULNESS

Mindfulness can help us to really notice the world around us. Living mindfully will help you to see all the good bits in life and appreciate the little things. It might sound fancy but it just involves paying attention to your actions and surroundings and really living in the moment. For example, why not try practising mindfulness at mealtimes? Turn off all your technology and really take notice of what you're eating, from the flavours on your tongue to the warmth in your stomach.

SELF-CARE

Sometimes being an adult means taking a day off from being an adult! Having a break helps you recharge mental energy. Whether your idea of a treat is ordering a takeaway when it's your turn to cook or bingeing on a TV series one afternoon, do what you want from time to time and don't feel too guilty that you're not at maximum productivity.

TALK TO A PROFESSIONAL

Even the biggest, baddest adults need a helping hand sometimes. Don't be afraid to talk to a healthcare professional if life is getting on top of you or your mental health has got too tricky for you to handle alone. Your GP can come up with a plan of action for you, talk through your options and put you in touch with the right people.

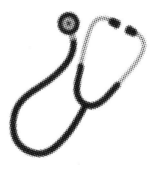

Adults need hobbies or else they are in danger of becoming boring. They have to be careful that they don't get overexcited about having the freedom to do nothing and end up doing nothing all the time. Keeping up at least one hobby gives adults a reason to leave the house, meet new humans and have new topics of conversation to enjoy, whether over wine and vol-au-vents or during a sweaty weightlifting session. However, there's no reason to drag one's lumpy grown-up body along to the opera if that's not and never will be your bag. Here are some hobby pairings you might prefer.

YOU LIKE: DRINKING

Hey, guess what? Adults like drinking too! They just disguise it as a hobby. First thing is to wave goodbye to the nights of getting crazy drunk with your besties. You can still do that, but you can't call it a hobby. Now, choose a favourite tipple for reasons that aren't simply 'it's the cheapest'. Do you like beer or wine, or do you prefer spirits? Once you've chosen, let's see what your options are:

Adulting on a budget

Country walks: When is daytime drinking acceptable? When you've walked more than three miles in the mud to do it! Country pubs are charming, cosy and the perfect setting to adultify your love of booze. There are plenty of walking routes available online, simply look one up, catch a form of public transport to your nearest patch of green and enjoy.

Volunteering: Many vineyards and some breweries rely on volunteers to help keep them running. Each volunteer usually works for anything from a day to a week and the work ranges from the boring (cleaning) to the back-breaking (picking grapes) but the pay comes in the form of wine/beer and sometimes meals. Some places abroad will give you free accommodation so you could even get a cheap week's holiday out of it!

Adulting with some fun money

Collecting: If you buy lots of different types of alcohol then people look at you strangely. But if you buy lots of one type of alcohol, you're a collector. Look out for special editions, new flavours and different brands. You can even turn a guilty pile of empties into quirky decorations by popping some LED lights inside or a candle on the top.

Tours: Many distilleries, breweries and vineyards offer tours of their business. The price varies wildly from place to place but information about how the drinks are made, a bit of history and at least one bevvy are often included in the price.

Posh adulting

Festivals: Boozy festivals are usually one- or two-day affairs, centred around one type of alcohol and also feature food and music. They're like music festivals, but you don't have to pretend you didn't get too drunk to see your favourite bands. As with tours, entry to these events varies in price but the costs can really rack up while you're there.

YOU LIKE: GETTING SWEATY

Where have all the endless summer afternoons gone? It can be pretty challenging to rustle up friends for a kickabout or to chase a Frisbee now you're all responsible and stuff. Instead you might have to get your fix of social sweatiness another way.

Adulting on a budget

Running: Once you get the initial outlay out of the way and you've bought your shoes, trews and tees, this is basically a free hobby. Apps can add a little spice to your efforts, whether you want to run from zombies, pit yourself against other users or simply create running routes in the shape of a willy.

YouTube classes: 'Darling, I swear by yoga', 'I simply can't live without Pilates' or 'If it's not barre I just don't want to know' are just some of the phrases you can annoy friends with if you take up YouTubercise. You don't have to dip into your hummus budget in order to access good quality, interesting classes, as you can do them at home. Perfect for the people who want to be healthy but not spend money or talk to other humans (basically all of us).

Adulting with some fun money

Clubs 'n' classes: If you like getting sweaty in company then clubs or classes are for you. There are two options: drop-in classes or buy a 'term'. Drop-in classes charge you only when you attend, so you can flex them to suit your budget but you might not always get a spot. Buying classes by the 'term' (a set number of weeks) is more common and usually works out cheaper in the long run, but you have to attend every week to get your money's worth! The options are pretty varied too – you can do all of your favourite sports and activities or get weird and try morning raves or cat yoga.

Bouldering/aerial: Both bouldering and aerial offer full body workouts with a little bit extra thrown in. Try bouldering if you like puzzle solving, as you build strength and mental agility during these rope-free climbing sessions. Aerial or circus classes are physically challenging but a lot of fun and are perfect if you like a little creativity with your exercise. Both activities are known for their excellent communities.

Posh adulting

Big races: If you're into a sport that features racing, such as cycling, swimming or running, there's likely to be a large-scale event that you can get mega-fit for. Big races take place all over the world – in the desert, on tropical islands, across mountains – and can be an amazing target to aim for in your training as well as a bit of a treat.

Extreme sports: What better way to experience the great outdoors than to catch a glimpse of it as you hurtle down a mountain at top speed, or cling to a cliff by your fingertips? If you agree with that statement, skiing or coasteering might be for you. Also consider base jumping, abseiling, underwater hockey and extreme ironing.

YOU LIKE: CULTURE

If you enjoy getting out of the house, seeing friends and experiencing some culture, daaahling, how about these apples?

Adulting on a budget
Museums/galleries: There are a heck of a lot of free museums and art galleries out there and it's almost criminal not to take advantage. Whether you're into art, fashion, history, science, the natural world – or anything! – there's likely to be a cheap or free museum nearby that will fascinate you.
Sketch crawls: If you'd like a low-commitment way to enjoy being creative and meet people, check online for

local sketch crawls and life-drawing classes. Sketch crawls usually meet once a month and feature a small walk around an area, stopping regularly to sketch a new scene (and for snacks!). Both crawls and classes usually involve a small fee but are a cheap way to entertain yourself.

Adulting with some fun money

Small shows: When you really pay attention you'll notice that your nearest town or city is buzzing with local theatre, touring troupes and independent productions. Keep an eye out for special 'seasons' and festivals that will up the amount of interesting stuff going on and take special notice of those flyers in the pub bathroom.

Special exhibitions: If a few trips to museums have whetted your appetite, keep an eye out for their stand-out exhibitions. Often focusing on one artist or cultural aspect, it can be a great way to springboard into a particular interest or find out more about something you were already quite interested in.

Posh adulting
Big gigs: If you feel like really putting on a top hat, there are some must-do cultural landmarks you, well, must do! Tick off this list: ِ

- See a symphony orchestra play classical music

- Watch a classical ballet

- Go to the opera

- Watch a Shakespeare play.

YOU LIKE: AWESOME DOCUMENTARIES

If you like nothing more than vegging on the sofa and having your mind blown, whether by beautiful views, crazy facts or hilarious chat via an insightful documentary, how about going out and immersing yourself in that world?

Adulting on a budget
Studio audience: If some of your favourite shows have studio audiences then you're in luck. You can sign up

online to be part of the audience. Search for your show with the term 'audience tickets'. Some shows over-issue tickets and admit people on a first come, first served basis, so make sure you get there with plenty of time to spare and have a plan B prepared.

Adulting with some fun money

Talks: If there's a subject that's piqued your interest, have a look for related talks in your area. You can listen to famous and well-qualified people talk about their experiences doing almost anything, from adventuring across the Himalayas to explaining the science behind travelling to Mars.

Fests: See above, but think on a larger scale. There are shows and festivals (of sorts) that gather top speakers, cutting-edge technological demonstrations and great merchandise stalls so you can spend the whole day immersed in another world.

Posh adulting

Adventure holidays: You don't have to just watch people do crazy things in beautiful places – you can do them too! There are all sorts of adventure holidays available, from backpacking tours to survival training weekenders. Whether you're looking to summit, plummet, paddle, hit the saddle, dive or survive, there is likely to be a course that suits you. Lots of companies create adventure packages, or you can simply search for your preferred activity in your chosen destination and see where that takes you.

CONVERSATION

Beware! The road to adulting is paved with many awkward silences. There will be countless occasions in your grown-up life when you'll have to make conversation with near or complete strangers: new jobs, meeting the in-laws, going to the hairdresser (the worst of all). The smile-and-nod technique will only get you so far so here are a few things to try when your cheek muscles start to hurt.

Magic mirror

People loooove talking about themselves. Ask lots of open-ended questions, such as 'What do you like to do?' or 'What have you been up to?' and watch that conversation train start rolling! Remember that the time for brutal honesty comes much (much) later in a relationship, so make interested noises and show that you understand and appreciate your chatting pal's point of view even if you don't agree.

Ears to the ground

Using the magic mirror technique is NOT permission to tune out of a conversation and reel through a set of planned questions. It's an earthly delight to be really listened to and we guarantee you'll score big if you really listen to what someone has to say, remember it and refer to it at a later time.

Minesweeping

We all love to get into a big fat juicy conversation, but when it comes to talking with strangers there are some 'Not now, Nigel' topics. Save the politics, religion, sex and tragedy for your besties and frenemies and stick to discussing last year's holiday with your new boss or your partner's lovely gran.

Peace out

If you've been caught at the buffet table by Chatty Uncle Gary and need to disengage before your sausages get cold, it might be easier than you think to make a getaway. 'Excuse me', when said with confidence, is adult code for 'I'm outta here.' If you need a little more bulk, try 'Excuse me, I must [INSERT TIME-SENSITIVE TASK HERE]'. Eating rapidly cooling sausages is one potential reason, as is grabbing a drink, visiting the bathroom or talking to someone before they leave. Finally, consider human sacrifice. No, not murder – it's never that bad. Simply include a new person in your conversation and verbally step back, allowing them to take on Chatty Uncle Gary while you make your escape.

HOSTING

Being a good host is basically like being a babysitter for grown-ups. You're in charge for the evening but if you do it right, the children (your guests) won't notice, they'll just think they had a fantastic time.

Invitations

Whether you're cooking a five-course tasting menu or just have a plate of biccies on the side, make it clear what will be on offer at your event. Be aware of timings – if you've invited friends over at lunchtime (12 noon–2 p.m.) or dinner time (5 p.m.–8 p.m.) then you should offer them at least a meal's worth of food.

Arrival

Take your guests' coats and offer them a drink. You should ideally have at least one soft drink, one alcoholic beverage and one hot drink available. It's impossible to overstress the importance of food here! If you are having a big meal later, have a few nibbles scattered around. If you are only offering light bites or snacks, supersize the nibbles. If you've mastered the art of decanting little bits of food into bowls then you've essentially mastered most of adulting.

The main event

Whatever your event is, have everything set up before your guests arrive. For example, if you plan on bingeing on a TV show, have the DVD to hand or ensure it's available via one of your streaming services. If you're serving a meal, prep as much as possible before your guests arrive so you don't spend too much time in the kitchen, away from them. Keep an eye on everyone's drinks and try to ensure no one's glass is empty for too long. If you have a group of guests that don't know each other very well then it's a good idea to keep up with the different conversations so you can rescue anyone caught by your more opinionated or brutally honest pals, or nudge your quieter friends towards the motormouths.

Oh no, things have gone wrong!
One of a host's main duties is being in charge of Plan B. For example, if your meal burns down the kitchen it's up to you to a) call the fire brigade, b) have a frustrated scream about the hours of wasted cooking and then c) suggest a few takeaway ideas. If there's a lull in conversation or the main activity is a bit of a dud, have a few alternative ideas in your back pocket. Maybe an easy game to play or a few conversational pointers (think more *Desert Island Discs* than Prime Minister's Questions).

THOSE TRICKY CONVERSATIONS

The formula for adulthood is you + short-term pain = long-term gain. This can mean having a painful conversation to improve your relationship instead of dodging the subject and leaving something to fester. Here's an incomplete list of conversations you can't swerve:

Are we in a relationship?   I'm sorry.

Have I upset you?

You have upset me.

I would like children/marriage/to move to Timbuktu, what about you?

I think this person/activity/ lifestyle is hurting you.

I effed up.   *I need help.*

MIND YOUR Ps AND Qs

There is no one-size-fits-all approach to having a productive and kind conversation about something that could be hurtful or challenging. However, there are some techniques you could use to help you be patient, understand and above all make the conversation effective and useful. Adults love an acronym, so we have whipped one up to help you remember: PLEASE.*

Plan

Go into the conversation knowing what you want to get out of it. For example, you might want some information, a confirmation or a change in behaviour. This will make it much easier to keep the conversation on track. Anything said that doesn't work towards that objective – for example, insults or a different problem – should be disregarded or sidelined for a different conversation.

Listen

It takes two people to have a conversation and although you may have worked things out in your head, the other person may have a whole different perspective on things. Don't use

---

*The PLEASE method works well with reasonable human beings. Occasionally you may find an absolute baddie who is fine with hurting you as long as it suits them. When you encounter these types of people, the PLEASE method will not work and disengaging or limiting contact is your best approach.

the time when the other person is talking to plan your next line of attack, actually listen and consider their words.

Empathise

You are not telling off a small child. You are not instructing a subordinate at work. You are not a hero versus a villain. You are talking to another human, probably one that you like very much and who has reasons for doing what they are doing. Even if they've been an absolute rotter to you, they will likely be surprised and defensive when they hear about it. Understanding their feelings and reasons for their actions doesn't mean you agree with them, but it will make them feel like a human being.

Ask

If you're feeling like you've reached a dead end and the other person isn't acknowledging this, asking them for their solution can open up the conversation. It turns the situation from you telling them off and getting your way to working together to make sure you are both happy. It can also be a great help for sulky pants: sometimes people on the defensive just say 'no' to every suggestion because they are hurt and feel attacked. Asking them for a solution gives them back some power while taking away their 'no, no, absolutely not' blocking method.

Silence

It's likely that silence will come up throughout the conversation. You'll both be grappling with challenging ideas and some tricky feelings, such as guilt or anger. If the other person needs a moment to think then let there be silence instead of using their befuddlement to press your point.

End

When the conversation is over, it's over. No after-chat sulking, no sly digs, no bad moods. This is easier said than done, so a physical action can sometimes help with the mental change. A sincere, lingering hug or cuddle can help. Or, if you're someone who holds on to feelings, leaving the room to make a cup of tea or grab something from the local shop can help you transition your mood.

If you think that **PLEASE** is going to be a lot to remember, this handy mantra is a shortcut to good communication. Before and during your challenging chat, keep this mantra in mind to help you focus.

Is it kind?
Is it true?
Is it necessary?

BODY

Recipes

Here's the thing: you're in charge of what you eat for the rest of your life now. You're going to be deciding what meals to have three times a day, 365 days a year, which is over 1,000 times a year.

Although ready meals and takeaways are convenient, they can get a bit samey after a while. But if you master a few essentials, you'll make your life much easier and your diet a lot healthier. Here are a few ways to take your cooking to the next level.

ADAPTABLES

You don't have to get lost in the details when deciding what to have to eat. How about just thinking of a flavour and whipping up a recipe from there? Sounds tricky? Here are a few starter packs of basic sauces and recipe ideas to get you started.

Classic tomato sauce

Serves 4

1 tbsp olive oil
2 garlic cloves, crushed or
chopped finely
400 g tin chopped tomatoes

1 tbsp tomato puree
1 tsp sugar
Salt and pepper to taste

Heat the oil and fry the garlic on a low heat for 1 minute.

Add chopped tomatoes, puree and sugar, and bring to the boil, then simmer for 5 minutes. Season.

This stores for 3–4 days in the fridge and up to three months in the freezer.

PIZZA

Serves 2

1 large pizza base, classic tomato sauce, handful of grated cheese, toppings of your choice

Spread the sauce on the pizza base, scatter over the cheese, add the toppings and cook for 12 minutes at 180°C (350°F).

BOLOGNESE SAUCE

Serves 4

1 onion, chopped, 1 pepper, chopped, 250 g minced beef, classic tomato sauce

Fry the veg and brown the meat, then add to the tomato sauce and simmer for 20–30 minutes.

WHITE BEAN STEW

Serves 4

400 g tin white beans, classic tomato sauce, crusty bread

Stir beans into sauce until heated through and serve with crusty bread.

CHICKEN/AUBERGINE PARMIGIANA

Serves 4

4 cooked chicken breasts/3 sliced and grilled aubergines, 1 ball mozzarella, sliced, classic tomato sauce, breadcrumbs

Layer the chicken/aubergine, mozzarella and sauce, ensuring there is enough sauce to cover the top. Add breadcrumbs and cook at 180°C (350°F) for 30 minutes.

Pesto sauce

Makes 1 jar

50 g pine nuts, 80 g basil, 50 g hard cheese, 150 ml olive oil, 3 garlic cloves

Dry fry the pine nuts in a small pan over a low heat until golden. Pour the nuts into a blender and add remaining ingredients. Whizz on a high speed until smooth. This stores for 5–7 days in the fridge and up to three months in the freezer.

PESTO SALMON

Serves 4

4 salmon fillets, pesto sauce, 150 g green beans with ends chopped off, 500 g new potatoes, butter to serve

Preheat oven to 180°C (350°F). Spread a thin layer of pesto on salmon fillets and cook for 20 minutes. Boil new potatoes for 10 minutes and green beans for 5 minutes. Serve and add a knob of butter to new potatoes.

PESTO PASTA

Serves as many as you want!

80 g dry pasta per person, pesto sauce, handful basil leaves, handful pine nuts

Cook pasta according to instructions on packet. Drain and return to pan, then add pesto. Stir until heated through and serve. Garnish with basil and pine nuts.

ONE-PAN PESTO POTATOES

Serves 2

300 g new potatoes, sliced, 150 g green beans with ends chopped off, 2 tbsp olive oil, pesto sauce, 1–2 eggs

Boil potatoes and beans for 5 minutes. Drain. Heat oil on low heat and add potatoes and beans. Cook for 8 minutes. Stir in pesto until warmed through. Make well in centre and crack in eggs, frying to your preference. Serve in pan.

Béchamel sauce

Serves 4

300 ml full-fat milk, 15 g butter, 15 g plain flour, 1 nutmeg

Bring milk to the boil and immediately reduce heat. In another pan, melt butter until bubbling. Add flour and quickly stir in, cooking for 1–2 minutes. Remove pan from heat and add milk gradually, stirring until smooth. Return to medium heat and bring to the boil, stirring constantly. Reduce to low heat and cook for around 5 minutes until sauce is thick and glossy. Season to taste with grated nutmeg.

SMOKY MACARONI CHEESE

Serves 4

320 g dry macaroni pasta, 150 g cheddar, grated, 1 tbsp chipotle paste, béchamel sauce

Cook the macaroni as per the packet instructions. Stir the paste and half of the cheese into the sauce. Put macaroni in an ovenproof dish and pour sauce over, stirring until everything is coated. Top with remaining cheese and grill until browned on top.

POTATO GRATIN

Serves 2

6 medium potatoes, peeled and thinly sliced, 2 balls mozzarella, grated, béchamel sauce, pepper to taste

Add most of the cheese to the sauce and stir over a low heat until melted. Mix with the potatoes and pour into an ovenproof dish. Top with remaining mozzarella and cook on 180°C (350°F) for 1 hour 10 minutes.

LASAGNE

Serves 4

200 g dry pasta sheets, béchamel sauce, bolognese (p.41), 150 g cheddar, grated

Line an ovenproof dish with a layer of pasta sheets, then béchamel, then bolognese, then a little of the cheese. Repeat twice. The final layer should be the rest of the pasta sheets, completely covered by the béchamel with the remaining cheese sprinkled over. Cook for 1 hour at 180°C (350°F).

MIX 'N' MATCH

One of the barriers to home cooking can be the idea that you have to buy a new round of ingredients for each meal – it's expensive and time-consuming. But that's fake news! Once you get the hang of a few basic recipes, like these ones, you can make a meal based on what's in your cupboard.

Stir-fry

Serves 4

Ingredients
2 tbsp oil, 250 g egg noodles

BASE

2 garlic cloves, crushed, grated thumb-sized piece ginger, 4 spring onions, sliced (optional), 2 chillies, sliced (optional)

VEG

300 g any combination of these vegetables (500 g if not using meat): onion (sliced), water chestnut, mange tout, mushroom (sliced), pepper (sliced), green beans, bean sprouts, carrots (peeled and sliced), baby corn, red chilli (sliced), edamame beans

MEAT

250 g any of these meats, cut into strips:
Pork, beef, chicken

SAUCE

1 pack of any of these sauces:
Szechuan, sweet chilli, hoisin, chow mein, sweet and sour

TOPPING

Handful sliced spring onion stalks, sesame seeds, cashew nuts

METHOD

Add the oil to a wok and cook over a high heat, until oil runs quickly and is starting to smoke.

Add base ingredients and cook for 1–2 mins, stirring constantly. Remove from wok.

Add meat and cook, stirring, until it is changed in colour but not fully cooked. Add vegetables and fry for a further 3 minutes (the stirring can't be overstated).

Add sauce and cook for 2 minutes. Meanwhile, cook the noodles as per the packet instructions.

Return the base ingredients to the wok, add noodles and warm through, then serve. Add toppings to bowls.

Curry

Serves 4

1 pack microwavable rice

BASE

2 tbsp oil, 2 garlic cloves, crushed, grated thumb-sized piece ginger, 1 onion, finely chopped, 1 tsp garam masala, 1 tsp turmeric, 1 tsp ground coriander, 1 tsp cumin

VEG

200 g any combination of these vegetables, 600 g if not using bulk: tomatoes, spinach, cauliflower florets, mushrooms (halved), green beans, peppers

BULK

400 g of one of these: chickpeas, parboiled potatoes, cooked chicken strips

SAUCE

Either of these combinations:
400 g tin tomatoes and 400 g coconut milk
2 x 400 g tins chopped tomatoes

TOPPING

Any of these flavour boosters: cubed paneer, chopped coriander, flaked almonds

METHOD

Heat oil and soften onions.

Add garlic, ginger and spices and cook for 1–2 minutes until aromatic.

Stir in bulk and vegetables, until coated and the veg have started to soften.

Add sauce and simmer for 30–45 minutes. Microwave rice just before serving.

Serve and add topping.

Herbs
WHAT SEASONING SHALL I USE?

ROSEMARY
Asparagus, broccoli, beef, ham, chicken

BASIL
Courgette, lettuce, mushrooms, peas, tomatoes, beef, lamb, mackerel, salmon

CORIANDER
Beetroot, mushrooms, tomatoes, lamb, ham, trout

SAGE

Broccoli, mushrooms, peas, pork, chicken

Beetroot, broccoli, green beans, lettuce, beef, lamb, chicken, trout, haddock

THYME

Garlic, steak, fish, chicken, potatoes

PARSLEY

TERMINOLOGY

Al dente - cooked until there is still a slight 'bite' to the texture, not completely soft

Baste - spoon hot liquid on to meat as it cooks

Beat - mix with spoon, rapidly, lifting the spoon high to incorporate as much air as possible

Blanching - dipping in boiling water and removing swiftly (around a minute)

Caramelising - cook slowly on a low heat until glossy, sometimes with sugar

Chop finely - cut into very small pieces

Chop roughly - cut into large, uneven pieces

Dice - cut into small, even cubes

Drizzle - sprinkle

Dry fry – fry without using oil

Fold – lightly mix ingredients by dragging spoon through middle of mixture and scooping up one side to 'fold' over to the other; should be done gently

Pare – peel the skin

Marinate – cover meat or vegetable in mixture and leave for some time

Poach – cook in hot but not boiling liquid

Reduce – cook liquid until thicker

Rounds – circular pieces

Sear – cook on high heat until outside is browned

Shallow fry – cook in a thin layer of boiling oil that partially covers the ingredients, turning often; also, sauté

Simmer – when liquid is bubbling but not yet boiling

There's no escaping it, exercise is a must-do part of adulting. It keeps your body fit, for which you'll only thank yourself as you get older, but has heaps of other benefits too, like releasing 'feel-good' endorphins and opportunities for socialising.

STRETCHING

You'll find the aches and pains increase as time goes by and incorporating a few stretches into your life can help you dodge them. Hold stretches for 10–15 seconds and stop if they are painful. As you are now very busy and important, you might find it easier to incorporate these stretches into your daily routine.

Getting out of bed

When you are out of bed, reach your arms up over your head. Keeping your hips stationary, lean to one side from the waist and hold. Repeat on the other side.

Brushing your teeth

Put one leg up on to a low ledge. This could be the toilet, the bath, the sink or a windowsill depending on your flexibility and bathroom layout. This stretch might be enough, but if you want to go deeper lean towards your foot. Repeat on the other side.

Bottom of the stairs

When you reach the bottom of the stairs, steady yourself against the wall with both hands and stand with your heels hanging off the edge of the step. Press down and hold. Repeat ten times.

Putting on your shoes

Stand with one foot half a metre in front of the other. Hinge at the hips and hold. Readjust if necessary to ensure your hips are facing forward and are at equal height. Repeat on the other side.

Watching TV

Sit on the floor with straight legs as wide as they will go. Lean forward from the hips and hold. Try to keep your knees pointing to the sky so your legs don't turn inwards. Release, and lean towards one foot and hold. Repeat on the other side.

FREE EXERCISE

Running

Even if all you have is a pair of trainers and some breathable clothes, you're ready to run. Running for half an hour, three times a week, is an excellent way to get in your prescribed dose of exercise.

Walking

Walking is low-intensity exercise but less daunting than running and much better than loafing on the sofa. Choosing to walk instead of driving somewhere can be a great way to start a positive change and sneak some exercise into your lifestyle.

Home workouts

You don't need expensive equipment to get sweaty at home. You can follow tutorials online or download some basic workouts. Even if you don't have much space, it is still possible to do anything from improving flexibility and core, through yoga or Pilates, to high-intensity exercises like burpees or skipping.

GROUP OR HOBBY EXERCISE

Not sure where to start? Take a look online to see if there are any local clubs or classes for any of the below:

- Badminton
- Basketball
- Circus skills
- Climbing
- Football
- Netball
- Pilates
- Rugby

- Spinning
- Squash
- Street dance
- Swimming
- Swing dance
- Tennis
- Trampolining

Where to look

A good place to start your search is online. Check out the classes advertised at your local college or a smaller gym for some cheaper options. If you know you're able to commit, it can be cheaper to sign up for a course of classes instead of attending drop-in sessions. Plus, not wanting to lose the money can be good motivation to go to every class!

First aid

Now that it's adulting time, it's good to know what to do in case of minor injuries. After all, Mum isn't around to kiss it better. However, if the injury is too serious or you're really worried, call a doctor.

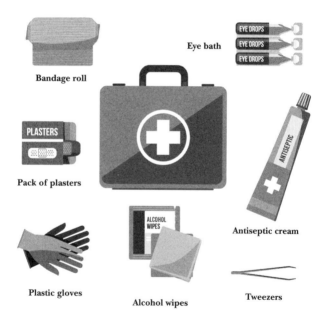

Bandage roll

Eye bath

Pack of plasters

Antiseptic cream

Plastic gloves

Alcohol wipes

Tweezers

OH NO! YOU HAVE...

Cut yourself deeply
Elevate the wound to stop the bleeding. Run it under cold water to clean and wrap it in a plaster or bandage, depending on the size of the wound.

Burnt yourself
Run the affected area under cold water for at least 10 minutes. If the affected area still feels warm, return it to the cold water. Loosely wrap in cling film or a plastic bag. Keep dressed for 24 hours.

Sprained a ligament
Stop what you're doing and, if it's a weight-bearing joint, sit down. Elevate the limb and cover in ice or a cooling pack until the swelling reduces (RICE is key: rest, ice, compression and elevation).

Fainted or felt faint
If you feel nauseous or as though you're going to pass out, lie down with your legs raised. If you can't lie down, sit with your head between your legs.

FINANCES

Bank accounts

Serious subject ahoy! Money matters and it will be both the key and the barrier to a lot of what you want to do in the future. This section will hopefully demystify a bit of the jargon around banking and money, and give you some tailored budgets to help you achieve (almost) everything you'd like to do.

CURRENT ACCOUNT

Current accounts are your garden-variety bank accounts. Most people will have access to a current account and it's usually the best account to use for most of your financial activity (and you HAVE to have one if you have a job). You can set up direct debits, withdraw money from and arrange overdrafts for current accounts. There are many types of current account, with some offering extra benefits for small fees, so look into what your bank offers.

SAVINGS ACCOUNT

A savings account is an account that can give you interest on the money you put in. It's usually not for day-to-day activity, so might not have a debit card attached and it's likely you will not be able to withdraw the money from cash machines.

ISA

A cash ISA is a type of savings account where you don't have to pay tax on the interest (you do with normal savings accounts). However, there is usually a limit to how much you can pay into it in a tax year.

BASIC ACCOUNT

If you have bad credit then you can set up a basic account. The rules are tighter than a normal account – no debit card or overdraft – so once you're out of money, you're out. Not all banks offer them, so talk to someone inside the bank about setting one up. However, you'll be able to use many of the normal functions of a bank account, like setting up direct debit payments. Plus, most basic accounts come with a top-up visa card you can transfer your money to, making it even easier for you to have a handle on how much you spend.

Credit cards

A credit card can help you make big purchases that you could generally afford but don't have the ready money for. They also help you build your credit score when you pay your monthly bills on time, which can benefit you when doing big grown-up things like buying a property. However, it's never free money and it's crucial you know what you're signing up for.

INTEREST-FREE CREDIT CARD

You always have to pay back a monthly minimum amount of what you owe on your credit card. Most cards charge you an extra sum each month as 'interest' on your debt. It's how they make money! Interest-free cards offer you the chance to not be charged that extra for a number of months.

0% BALANCE TRANSFER

Generally, credit cards charge a fee when you use them like debit cards, e.g. when you transfer money between accounts. However, 0 per cent balance transfer cards waive this fee, which is useful if you need to pay someone back a large sum or want to transfer your existing credit card debt for a better interest rate.

LOW APR

APR means 'annual percentage rate' and is what you should look at when you're trying to see how much interest you'll be paying on your credit card debt. Low APR cards have low interest rates (great!) but as credit card vendors are always trying to make money, they often have high fees and penalties for late payments.

Savings and budgets

Budgets aren't just for the government! (That's a joke for adults. It's the perfect mix of cheesy and boring. You'll be experiencing a lot of those now you're a sophisticated old person.) Back to real talk: life is so much easier when you know how much money you have coming in and how much you have going out. Imagine not having a week of sweating bullets before payday! A bit of ready cash for treats. Some savings set aside for big purchases.

Having some money set aside is one of the best things you can do for yourself. There is no situation in life that doesn't need a bit of extra cash. Walking the traditional path of adulthood? You'll be looking at buying a house and getting married. Want to get away from it all? You need a few notes to start new somewhere else. Things have gone horribly wrong? At least you don't have to worry about money for a little while. Save, save, save!

WTF (WHERE'S THE FUNDS?)

It's useful to know what your savings are for, so you can keep that in mind if you are tempted to spend them.

Having savings goals can also really help to motivate you because you're not just adding to a total, you're working to get something.

Permanent savings

Having long-standing savings is one of the best things you can do for Future You. These are 'rainy-day' savings, or to give them their proper name, 'Look, One Day You're Going to be Too Old to Work and Then What?' savings. They can also be dipped into for emergencies like exploding washing machines or unexpected home moves. A normal savings account is best for these.

Special savings

There are some things in life that need saving up for, like a deposit for a home, a new car or a big holiday. Instead of taking out big loans or credit plans, squirrel away some money. It takes longer, but there's less risk of debt. A cash ISA can be good for this, as you're unlikely to max out their limits and there are better interest rates (so, free money).

Premium Bonds

Premium Bonds are a kind of savings account that swap interest for the chance to win cash prizes. Each bond is £1 and you must buy £100 minimum to start your saving. You may withdraw your money at any time and while it is in bonds it earns no interest. However, once a month each bond is entered into a prize draw and you have the opportunity to win tax-free cash prizes, at the odds of 24,500 to 1. If inflation increases while your money is in bonds, and you don't win any prizes, you'll have lost out (this is statistically the most likely scenario). However, the cash prizes range from £25 to £1 million, so there is also the chance you'll increase your money.

Lifetime ISA

You can add up to £4,000 a year to a Lifetime ISA and the government will add a yearly 25 per cent bonus to what you put in. This will be up to £1,000 a year! However, any withdrawals come with a 25 per cent fee, unless it's to buy a house, and you can't add any more money after the age of 50. It's the perfect way to save for a house, although only use it if you won't need to access that money for any other reason.

WHICH BUDGET IS FOR YOU?

You might think that being on a budget means you can't spend anything, but that's not the case. A budget is simply a plan for how you spend your hard-earned cash. As you are in charge of your own life now, you can switch around your budget at any time to better suit your life goals and interests.

The Just Surviving budget

Most adults face a time in their life when they have to live from payday to payday. It doesn't mean you're failing at adulting, it just means you're doing what you have to in order to get through. A Just Surviving budget says 'stuff it' to the savings and 'pah!' to paying your debts, and focuses on the most important thing – paying the bills.

Sit down with a pen and paper and work out your monthly income after tax. Deduct all essential bills from it (rent, energy, water, council tax, phone, etc.). What you have left is your spare cash or, for now, 'survival money'. The bulk should go on food, with a small percentage set aside for unexpected expenses like new shoes.

The Kill All Debt budget

This is for people with some lump sums hanging over their heads. It might be daunting or even a downer to take a steely look at your debt, but this will help you in the long run. It's pretty similar to the Just Surviving budget, but allows for a little extra room to spend. Include your minimum monthly payments in your spare cash calculations. Now look at your remaining spare cash. What's the most you can divert back to the debt from that? A starting guideline might be to spend 25 per cent on food, 25 per cent on fun and 50 per cent on paying your debts. Ideally, if you find that's a bit too much on food or fun, divert the excess to the debt.

The Special Savings budget

Want to make a big purchase or just spend responsibly? Make your spare cash calculations. Now arrange for all bills to go out via direct debit shortly after payday. Look at your spare cash sum and divide it into portions: one for fun and food, and another for savings. Instead of keeping your savings in your bank account, ripe for using for those 'little treats', set up a direct debit to send that to a savings account. Now you can't touch it without some effort!

The Planning (Retirement) budget

If you are in full-time employment, your employer will have set you up with a pension, in which case you'll already be spending a chunk of your income on your retirement before it even hits your bank account. But if you'd like to have an additional rainy day pot, try this budget. Treat your extra pension like it's a bill and set up a direct debit to go out to a savings account at the same time your other bills go out. Ten per cent of your spare cash is a good amount to start with, but try to increase the proportion every time your pay increases.

Bills, bills, bills

Aside from love, has any subject been written about so much as paying the bills? No one likes it, everyone has to do it. But what's the best way for it?

SET UP DIRECT DEBITS AND BILL PAYMENTS

Every time you have a new type of bill to pay, try to set up a direct debit as close to payday as possible. That way, the money leaves your account without you having to think about it (and potentially forget to pay the bill). It also means it's harder for you to overspend and miss a payment.

If your income is variable or unreliable, direct debits may not be the way forward for you. You may not have the cash at the same time each month, but the direct debit will come out regardless and you could be hit with overdraft fees. You may need to use another approach to stay on top of bills. A monthly or weekly alarm on your phone should get your attention, or perhaps flagging some days in your electronic calendar. There are apps that send automatic reminders and there's even ye olde wall calendar for those who stay true to the old school.

WORK

2# *Getting a job*

Here's a fact: if you are in full-time employment until you retire, you will spend around a third of your life in work. Here's a guess: you, specifically you reading, probably need to work in order to be able to afford a roof over your head and to put food in your belly. Here's a saying: you can either work to live or live to work. It's entirely up to you whether you are passionate about your job and pour your life into it, or whether you power through your day knowing it enables you to invest in the things you truly love. There's no right or wrong way to feel. But no matter how you feel, you're going to be spending a lot of time at work and there are a few right and wrong ways to act...

The best way to look for a job depends on lots of factors, including the industry you'd like to work for and the stage you're at in your career. General advice isn't much help here, other than to say there is no such thing as too much research. We wise old masters of adulting are also going to assume that you young grasshoppers are at least trained in life up to yellow belt. You arrive at interviews on time, in shoes instead of flip-flops and don't text during your appointment. If you are a no to any of these, please see

the prequel book, *How to Open Doors and Other Challenges.**
However, there are a few ways you can take your job-
securing abilities to the next level.

*This is not a real book, sorry!

BE INTERVIEW CONFIDENT

There's something that only comes with experience and
certain financial situations – and that's a sense of self-
worth as an employee. A lot of people endure their first
one or two rounds of interviews with cheerful desperation;
all gratitude towards their employer and a medium sense
of self-loathing towards themselves (sample thought of the
first-time employee: 'How can you employ me, I barely
managed to put my clothes on the right way round this
morning?!'). It takes working a few jobs to realise a) your
employer also only just managed to put their clothes on the
right way round this morning and b) you are allowed and
deserve to have opinions and preferences as an employee.
You'll eventually realise that both you and your prospective
employers are in the spotlight when it comes to interviews.

They are a great opportunity to find out vital information about the company and you can also show yourself off a bit at the end when you are asked if you have any questions (if the interviewer does not offer this opportunity, see it as a red flag).

LIVE-TO-WORK Qs

If a career or loving what you do is really important to you then you'll want to know more details about the job role and any development opportunities.

Is there room in the role for growth and advancement?

You might be nervous to ask a question like this in case you give the impression you're looking to move out of the role before you have it! But job growth doesn't just mean promotion, it means training in specialist knowledge, taking on extra responsibilities and adding variety to your role.

What would a typical work week look like?

Job adverts often list a variety of tasks that you will be expected to tackle. The questions you will have answered should have made clear which tasks in particular they're looking for you to work on, but this is a great opportunity to make sure the job you've applied for lines up with your career aspirations.

How could I impress you in the first three months?/ What are your expectations for this role in the first 60 days?
The first version of the question is a bit more ballsy, so if you don't feel ready to be that flashy then use the second question to get your information. But if you're up for it, this could be a really great question to ask! You'll know just what to do when you get the role and you will have signalled to the interviewers that you are a keen candidate.

WORK-TO-LIVE Qs

If you aren't necessarily interested in the work itself then the company culture and your colleagues really become important. You'll want to combine one of these questions with a general query, so you don't sound too suspicious of this work malarkey.

Is overtime expected?

This is another one that might seem a little pushy. But your time is one of your most valuable resources and you'll need to know how the company you work for intends to spend it. Overtime isn't necessarily a bad thing – if it's paid then you could very well do with the extra pennies – and if your interviewers get offended by your asking then you will know they're not transparent employers.

What is the culture of the company?

Is it important that you get on well with your colleagues and that there will be fun non-work elements to your day? Or would you prefer to reserve your personal energy for your personal life and not partake in any extracurriculars? If you ask about the culture you'll get this kind of important information.

GENERAL Qs

These questions will weed out information that is useful to know regardless of your working style. If you're looking to combine general queries and work-to-live queries: the first query of each section work well together and using the second query of each section nicely balances interest in work and interest in company culture.

What do you like about working here?
As the old saying goes, when in doubt crack this one out. You'll be able to tell if the interviewer is able to easily answer the question (are there long pauses or is it a fluent answer?) and this should give you an idea of whether what is good about a company fits with your personal taste.

What are the biggest challenges facing this department at the moment?
This is a polite way of asking about some of the downsides of the role. No job is without its cons, even dream jobs, and it's better to be prepared. You may even be able to go into the job with some ideas on how to tackle these challenges, although it's probably better to have completed your first week before you launch your interdepartmental reshuffle.

NEGOTIATING

You don't have to be the modern-day Albert Einstein to be worth something to a company. As you spend longer working you'll experience the other side of hiring and see just how tricky it is to find someone who works well and fits in with the company. So don't be afraid to negotiate. However...

DON'T negotiate at the interview. You haven't got the job yet!

DO put your requests in context. Refer to the salary not reflecting the requirements of the role, for example.

DON'T try to negotiate without having done your research. Simply saying, 'I want more money because I want more money' won't cut it.

DO talk about precedent. Mention the average wage of people in your role in your area, if that would be helpful, or discuss the incentives that your current company offers, such as flexitime.

DON'T be demanding or rude. Rude is how insecure people act confident and it won't get you what you want.

DO accept no for an answer. The company should be pretty forthcoming with whether they can meet your requirements. It's OK to haggle with them once they enter negotiations but if they say they can't meet some or any of your requests, stop negotiating and decide whether you want or need the job as it is offered.

CONTRACTS

Congratulations! You've got the job. Pour yourself a glass of something tasty and get out the blankets because it's time to curl up with some fascinating reading material: your contract. First thing's first, your new company should give you ample time to read and sign your contract. This is a legally binding document so both you and your new employer should be taking this part very seriously. What should you look at to ensure you've done your part?

Pink Floyd

The first thing to check is your Pink Floyds, 'money' and 'time'. Are the salary and the hours what you agreed? Your hours shouldn't exceed 48 hours a week and a company should only ask you to opt out of the 48-hour working week if your role requires bouts of travel or if you work for certain professions, such as the emergency services or a shift worker. Are you paid overtime?

Notice me!

How much notice are you required to give, or be given, before your contract is terminated? Normal amounts run between one and three months. If you have only a few weeks' notice then you'll be at a disadvantage if the company decides to turf you out. Too much notice and you'll have trouble finding a new company that can wait for you to start.

Off days

What will your holiday pay, sick pay and maternity or paternity pay be? How many days do they offer? Are there any special provisions? For example, some companies only pay sick leave once you have been off for five days and can provide a doctor's note. When does the company's 'year' start? Some leave allowances are January to December, others roll with the financial year.

What it says on the tin

No matter how the job was advertised, the description included in your contract or written statement will be the one you are held to (legally!). This is your last chance to check that the job you are taking on will be what you thought and to clarify vague lines such as 'will be required to take on other tasks as appropriate'.

RIGHTS AT A GLANCE

Your working rights are largely formed by your contract, which is why it's so important to read the whole thing! You also have basic legal rights, which both your contract and your actual working conditions must conform to. If you have a job with special requirements, such as shift work or night work, your rights may differ and you should do extra research on what you're entitled to.

This information is correct as of April 2018.

National minimum wage for people aged 18–20 is £5.90

National minimum wage for people aged 21–24 is £7.38.

National minimum wage for people aged 25 and over is £7.83.

Workers can take one uninterrupted 20-minute break if they work more than 6 hours a day.

Companies are not required to pay for rest breaks.

Companies do not have to offer paid sick leave other than statutory sick pay.

Workers are entitled to statutory sick pay, which is currently £89.35 per week for up to 28 weeks and starts after the worker has been off for at least four days.

Full-time workers are entitled to at least 28 days' paid holiday. Companies can include bank holidays in that allowance. There are currently eight bank holidays a year.

Part-time workers are entitled to the same rates as full-time workers for holiday and sick pay, pension opportunities (they are entitled to the same rate of pay for holiday, sick leave and pension but the total amount will reflect their reduced hours), the same access to training opportunities and the same right to promotion, transfer or redundancy.

Statutory maternity leave can be up to 52 weeks. The first 26 weeks is known as ordinary maternity leave and you have the right to return to your old job at the end of this period. The second 26 weeks is known as additional maternity leave and your employer may change the conditions of your return.

Workers may be entitled to shared parental leave, which is offered to parents of any gender. Check the gov.uk website for full details.

UNIONS

You may want to join a union during your working life. Unions can seem pretty scary but you don't have to be in trouble with your company to need them. After all, companies have all sorts of access to lawyers and knowledge of employment law that the ordinary bod simply doesn't. Sure, unions can be on your side if you and your company come into conflict, but they can also just offer advice and get you up to speed with your rights.

All for one!

There are plenty of pros to being in a union. As mentioned, there's the access to information. Union reps can also come and be on your 'team' in big meetings concerning pay or health and safety. It can be pretty scary facing up to a group of senior staff on your own so a union member can help you avoid being railroaded. If your workplace is unionised this helps you act as a team with your other colleagues, so when you bring your issues to your bosses your ideas are united and your voice is strong. This united front will help you have a stronger negotiating point.

Unions have a reputation for being politically active but you don't have to go on lots of marches to be in one. You do, however, have to pay fees.

One for all?

Research shows that unionised workers are paid around 12 per cent higher wages than their non-union counterparts. However, it just wouldn't be adulting if we didn't look at both sides of the story. Union workers have to pay mandatory fees to the union. Although these costs are often scaled to your wages, you may feel you just can't spare the cash. Part of a union's power comes from its ability to call many different workers to act as one, which will have a bigger impact on a company than if just one worker were to fight a cause. There can also be a con for some union members – they may be required to act in a way they don't agree with. Because their power comes from democracy, unions can even be hobbled by this, as they are tied up by internal arguments on how to act on an issue.

How to survive your colleagues

If you thought being forced to hang out with your best friend's awful boyfriend was bad, just wait until you get to work! You will spend your whole life working with awful and annoying people that seem to exist just to thwart you. But here's the secret about awful and annoying people: you're one too! Even if you are a rainbow child who rescues cats from trees as a hobby, there is going to be someone out there who writhes with rage because you make a strange noise when you drink your tea. (Note: this is just an example, you the reader may be a perfectly perfect tea drinker.) You are not required to be best friends with all of your colleagues, but even the most nasal-voiced pen-clicking co-worker deserves your respect and professional courtesy.

EXCEPTIONS

There are a few exceptions to this peace-to-all approach. If your work is being seriously hampered by a colleague or if you feel at all harassed, threatened or bullied by a colleague, please talk to a manager. It is important that you should be able to work to the best of your ability and it is so, so, so important that you are never deliberately made to feel crummy at work.

MAKE
THE
TEA

SERIOUSLY, MAKE THE TEA

HOME

Finding the right place for you

Sure, sure, we all live in a place we call home, but there's living and then there's *living*. It's possible for you (yes, you!) to live in a home that looks like it should be in a magazine or on Pinterest. All it takes is a little planning, a little regular work and some adulting knowledge.

RENTING

Viewing a home

We've all been the awkward renter poking our nose around a flat while the letting agent smiles and vaguely threatens that 20 other people are desperate to take it. We look, but do we see? Here's a handy checklist to make sure you don't end up living in a soggy studio flat with a toilet/kitchen combo.

What needs to work

These are essentials that need to be right before you make an offer on a property. Plus checking them gives you something to do instead of circling the room for the fourth time.

- Doors – do they close?

- Shower – what's the water pressure like?

- Toilet – no one wants a slow flusher. Ask whether the toilet uses a macerator. They're used when the toilet isn't attached to an outside wall and make ugly noises when flushing and sometimes when doing nothing at all!

- Oven – do all the hobs work? Does the oven work?

- Taps – are they leaking?

- White goods – if they're included, are they set to the right temperature?

- Walls – are they mouldy or damp to touch?

- Windows – do they close and what glazing are they? If they're single glazed you'll spend more on heating.

- Bedroom – what will your quality of sleep be? You may struggle if the roads outside are noisy. Stand by the bed for a moment and listen.

WHAT'S THE RIGHT HOME FOR YOU?

Aside from it having a minimum of four walls, a bedroom and a toilet, do you even know what sort of home you'd like? If you've been skipping over the letting agent's descriptions of flats and just circling those in the right budget, this could help you decide where you really want to live.

Green fingers

Do you want to try your hand at gardening? If you love picking herbs from the garden for dinner or sitting outside surrounded by flowers, you need to focus on outside space. First requirement – have a garden! Second requirement – have a south-facing garden, as they get the most light.

Foodie

You're going to need lots of worktop and cupboard space and an ample fridge and freezer. Try to keep in mind your kitchen gadgets when looking, as they can quickly fill the worktop space. Plug points in the kitchen are going to be another thing to look out for.

Homebody

You need to take a hard look at the living room. Is there enough space for sofas, are there plenty of plug points for electronics, and how much light does it get in the daytime? South-facing windows get the most light, which is perfect for weekends.

Hoarder

You need LOTS of storage space or space for your storage space! Are there inbuilt cupboards and shelves? Are there lots of corners to squeeze shelving units and storage boxes into? Remember that hallways are often a good source of untapped storage.

Your kitchen – the essentials

Your kitchen is where a lot of your adulting magic is going to happen, so you need to have more than a pot to pestle in. Make sure you not only have the right equipment but are also able to maintain it.

MUST-HAVE EQUIPMENT

The basics

We're going to assume that you already own the holy trinity of cookware: saucepans, frying pans and oven trays. The better you get in the kitchen, the more you'll need these to come in different sizes and depths. You should have a set of scales, a spatula and a couple of wooden or silicone spoons. If there is ONE kitchen tip you need to know it is to always keep your knives sharp! A sharp knife does the work twice as well and in half the time. Plus as it goes in easier it's less likely to slip on the food and cut you.

Next level

These are your next-level equipment items. You'll need these to make *Masterchef*-standard meals.

Thermometer　　　**Blender**　　　**Tongs**

Juicer　　　**Ladle**　　　**Potato masher**

Whisk　　　**Springform cake tins**　　　**Pizza cutter**

Steamer　　　**Heatproof oven dish**　　　**Measuring spoons**

Expert-level equipment

- Pestle and mortar

- Knife sharpener

- Garlic crusher

- Stew pot

- Cast-iron skillet

- Griddle pan

- Separate cutting boards for meat, vegetables and bread

Crockery

How many people live in your home? Double the number for your ideal number of plates, glasses and cutlery. That buys you one lazy washing-up day or means you're sorted if you want to have a few friends round.

WASHING-UP

	Sponge	Cloth	Washing-up brush	Wire wool	Washing-up liquid	Dishwasher
Stainless-steel cutlery	✓	✓	✓	✓	✓	✓
Non-stick pans (e.g Teflon pans)	✓	✓	✗	✗	✓	✗
Cast-iron pans	✓	✓	✓	✗	✗	✗
Enamel cast-iron pans	✓	✓	✗	✗	✓	✗
China	✓	✓	✓	✗	Mild	Check instructions
Crockery	✓	✓	✓	✓	✓	✓
Glassware	✓	✓	✓	✗	✓	✓

Your garden
_ the essentials

Hitting adulthood is a lot like hitting puberty, except instead of becoming interested in sex you become interested in garden centres (and not just to look at the fish). Accept the inevitable and check out some of these handy garden maintenance tips.

MUST-HAVE EQUIPMENT

Small gardens
Trowel
Hand fork
Secateurs
Gardening gloves
Watering can

Big gardens
Shovel
Spade
Rake

Lawn gardens
Lawnmower
Edge trimmer

SEASONS

SPRING

Dig out mess, e.g
stones, weeds, old plants
Plant bulbs and seedlings
Flowers bloom

Harvest fruits
and vegetables
Plant trees, hedges and
winter vegetables
Remove dead annuals

AUTUMN

SUMMER

Harvest fruits
and vegetables
Water on dry days
Weed weekly
Fend off pests
Flowers bloom

Harvest winter vegetables
Prune shrubs
Maintain soil with compost

WINTER

HOW TO PLANT A PLANT

 Dig a small hole in the soil, a little deeper and wider than the roots of your plant.

 Gently massage the roots of the plant to loosen them.

 Place the plant in the hole and fill with compost around the base of the plant and the roots until they are firmly encased and covered.

 Water, to give it a little 'welcome home' love.

WHAT SHOULD YOU PLANT?

Some plants are no-fuss growers and others need to be whispered words of encouragement 24 hours a day. If this is your first try at maintaining a garden, you might want to start with some of these easy plants.

Growbag vegetables
If your back garden is paved over or if you don't have much space, growbags can be a good cheat. Simply cut evenly spread large holes for each plant and water regularly. Here are some of the vegetables you can grow in them:

+ Tomatoes

+ Cucumbers

+ Aubergines

+ Sweet peppers

+ Chilli peppers

+ Courgettes

Herb gardens

Herbs do well in pots and containers and are pretty versatile as long as they are kept in nice and sunny surroundings. Some prefer wet soil and others prefer well-drained soil (put a layer of stones at the bottom of their pots and don't overwater), so check their packets for more information. Here are some of the herbs you can grow in pots and containers:

- Mint
- Basil
- Parsley
- Sage
- Bay
- Thyme
- Rosemary

Bedroom

Ah, the boudoir! This is where all the magic happens. Unless you like to have a cheeky quick one on the living room sofa? I'm referring to sleep of course! Although science doesn't fully understand sleep, it knows enough to know it's important. The ideal adulting bedroom is clean, tidy and an oasis for snoozing the night away.

SHEET, SON!

Most people would rather fist fight an alligator than change their bed sheets and who can blame them? Alligators are notoriously bad boxers thanks to their small arms. But change the bed sheets you must. You (should) spend eight hours a night in those sheets and by the end of the week they are chock-full of dead skin cells, grease, sweat and maybe even a little bit of dribble. If you were on your best behaviour, you would change your sheets once a week. Once every two weeks is still OK and you won't die if you only change them once a month. If you leave it any longer than that though, you are officially gross.

LIGHTS OUT

You're an adult now and if you want to fulfil your childhood dream of having a television the size of a wall so you can play video games in bed, I cannot stop you. I will, however, recommend that you turn it off at least half an hour before you go to bed. You need 30 minutes of screen-free time before you go to sleep to help your eyes and brain calm down after processing so much information. You can also help yourself by having an alarm clock, instead of your phone – so you can leave your phone to charge in another room, ensuring you aren't interrupted in the night by alerts.

Your bathroom – the essentials

Your bathroom is simultaneously the cleanest and the dirtiest room in the house. You go in there dirty, you come out clean. The hard shiny surfaces that make up most bathrooms are hostile to bacteria, which is good, but very friendly to dust and grime, which is bad. The bright side is that they are very easy to clean. Oh, there's nothing so fun as wiping down a tap, watching it go from splotchy and toothpaste-encrusted to shiny and fresh. (Yes, as an adult, this is now your idea of fun. Assimilate.)

NO SHAME

It's pretty likely that you will be sharing your bathroom at least some of the time and there are a few items that you can have on hand to ensure there's no embarrassment to be had.

Discreet smelly spray – you know you poo. You know everyone else poos. But you don't need to know there's been a poo, you know?

Back-up toilet roll – imagine your poor mother's face if she comes to visit and she has to call through the toilet door for you to hand over more toilet roll, because you haven't got an extra roll tucked discreetly by the dispenser.

A hand towel – now we are adulting we wipe our hands on a hand towel, not our trousers. Change it once a week or risk it becoming so full of little life forms you have to start charging it rent.

A small, lined bin – this should be within reach of your toilet. Sanitary items shouldn't be flushed down the toilet and it will also be a handy disposal point for non-recyclable packaging.

FIGHT THE GOOD FIGHT

Mould is going to be your number one nemesis in the bathroom because it's such a warm, humid area. You need to be the Batman of the bathroom, ever fighting the forces of darkness that threaten to take over your domain. Hang your bathmat on the radiator or the side of the bath if you have one, to ensure that it dries swiftly. Chuck it in the washing machine every few weeks with some of your towels. Move your product bottles when cleaning your washing area, especially if they sit in the bath or shower. Mould and dirt will flock to where they are. Bathrooms are also one of the few places where you have to regularly clean the walls, and even ceilings, especially if you don't have a window in there. The damp can cling to these and cause mould.

How to frou-frou your living room

If decanting food into bowls is half of adulting, adding a couple of nice cushions to your living room is the other half. If you want to transcend to a god-level adult, buy a couple of throws and blankets that coordinate with the cushions, fold them and have them draped over your sofa or stacked on a box. An added plus: you'll have a blankie on hand for the cold evenings!

Long-held adulting wisdom says to take down your film and music posters and put up framed art, but we don't want to cramp your style. Simply pop your posters in frames and voila! Sophistication. (Geek artwork or alternative designs do look a little smarter than your average contemporary poster though.) The 'add a frame to it' method works well with all sorts of things – postcards are cheap and come in all sorts of amazing designs.

Finally, consider the pot plant. Keeping a non-succulent pot plant alive for more than six months is the first gateway to adulthood. Instead of relying on your potentially patchy instinct on how to maintain it, look up the type of plant and set up a reminder on your phone for when you need to water it.

Fixing broken things

Things are going to go wrong and when they do you can either spend time or money on them. If you'd like to spend money, go right ahead and contact a professional. If you want to save your pennies and look like a bit of a guru to your friends, master some of these DIY basics.

THE DIY MANUAL

Change a lightbulb

Make sure the light switch is off (seriously, you don't want to get zapped). Unscrew or twist slightly to release the lightbulb. Take it with you to buy a replacement, paying special attention to the wattage and type of fitting it uses (bayonet, Edison screw cap, spotlights, etc.).

Fix a leaky pipe

Most leaky pipes are caused by an aged washer, which is the rubber ring that sits between the pipe and the fixture. You can find cheap replacements at most hardware stores. Turn the water off at the pipe. There should be a water shut-off valve that does this, usually found on the inside of your house on the side closest to the street. Place a bucket under the pipe because when you unscrew it all the leftover water is going to come gushing out. Replace the washer and pop the pipe back into place.

Paint a wall

If you've put up a lot of pictures or had a few too many parties, you may need to give your place a fresh coat of paint. Before you start, place masking tape along the edges of walls so you don't accidentally paint the ceiling, floor or skirting boards. When painting a wall use a wide roller brush for the best texture. Don't roll up and down, but in a close V shape, otherwise you will see the stroke marks.

Fill in holes in walls

If you need to fill in small or medium holes, buy some wall filler or expanding foam. Squeeze the filler into the area and wait for it to dry. Once dry, sand down until level with the wall, then paint over it.

Bleed a radiator

The most common cause of squiffy heating is a radiator full of air. You'll need to go all Dracula and bleed it to fix it. This sounds goulish and complicated, but is actually satisfying and easy. You'll need a radiator key, which costs less than a pound in most shops. Turn the heating off. Have a bowl and a towel ready in case the radiator is not full of air and it spurts water all over you. Fit the key over the bolt at the top of your radiator and turn it until you can hear air hissing out. Once it starts to make a bubbling noise, shut it off.

CLEANING

Clean your house you filthy animals! Don't you want to be able to look at the floor in the kitchen and not see a rundown of last week's meals? Wouldn't you like to be able to pick up something from the shelves without having a dusty sneezing fit?

Clothes

Before you clean your house, you should also clean your person. We're going to make the assumption that you know how to wash yourself (don't forget your feet, your legs and between your bum!) and focus on your clothes.

The basics

Washing machines are a bit like spaceships but a few rules apply no matter how hi-tech they are. Powder goes in the washing machine drawer or drum. Liquid goes in the washing machine drawer, or drum if the package comes with a holder. Tabs go in the washing machine drum. Most things can be washed at 30°C, which is the most environmentally friendly setting, but dirt and stains will need a higher setting.

Fabric	Washing	Drying	Ironing	Warning!	How often?
Cotton and linen	All temperatures	Line dry, tumble dry	High heat	Don't use bleach.	After every wear if worn next to your skin. 4–5 wears if a suit or jacket.
Wool and cashmere	Cold water or hand-wash	Line dry	No	Don't use bleach. Don't use fabric conditioner. Sometimes dry cleaning is recommended, check labels.	After every wear if worn next to your skin. Wool every five wears. Cashmere every two wears.
Denim	Cool water – 30°C	Line dry, tumble dry	No need	Don't use bleach. Colour can bleed in warm water.	Every 5–6 wears.
Silk, and silk blends	Cold water, hand-wash or 'delicate' setting	Line dry	Low heat	Don't use bleach. Don't use fabric conditioner.	After every wear if worn next to your skin. Every 2–3 wears.
Polyester and nylon	All temperatures	Line dry, tumble dry	Medium to low heat	Don't use bleach	After every wear if worn next to your skin. Every 5 wears.

NEXT LEVEL

Bio vs non-bio

Biological detergent is more powerful, containing enzymes that break down grease and starch. This means it's great for tackling food and general stains.

Non-biological detergent does not contain these enzymes and works better on a slightly hotter cycle. Although not as good at stain removal, non-bio is best if you have sensitive skin.

EXPERT LEVEL

Separate colours

If you want your whites and colours to stay as bright and/or white as possible, it's best to wash them separately from your darker clothes. Even when you can't see any obvious staining after washing, some dye does inevitably come out during the wash. Do your washing in three batches; whites, darks and colours for the best results.

Delicates

Ooh la la, we are talking lingerie! But this also applies to anything fiddly, beaded, embellished or, well, delicate. These items can easily get caught up in the hurly-burly of the washing cycle, catch on other bulkier clothes and tear. Buy a little mesh bag and pop your delicates in there before putting them in the wash.

Clean home, clean mind

Now you yourself are sparkling, turn your attention to the world around you. First, let's tool up.

EQUIPMENT

Bathroom
Anti-bacterial spray
Glass cleaner
Small fibre cloth
Dry cloth
Mop

Toilet
Bleach
Toilet brush

Kitchen
Anti-bacterial spray
Hob/oven cleaner
Small fibre cloth
Mop

Wood or lino floor
Dustpan and brush
Mop

Carpet
Vacuum
Carpet cleaner

Wooden furniture
Duster
Soft cloth

WHAT TO DO

Despite how some moaners make it sound, adult life isn't really work, clean, sleep. For a hygienic house that's sure to impress visiting relatives, try to do the basics weekly, incorporate the next-level stuff every other week and tackle the expert-level bits every few months.

The basics

- Hoover, wipe the surfaces, mop hard floors.

- Bleach toilet, clean shower and sinks (including draining board) with product.

- Wipe hobs and splash panel.

Next level

- Buff mirror and glass with dry cloth, wipe skirting, scrub toilet with toilet brush.

- Run duster along surfaces that you don't usually take notice of, like cut designs on doors, rails and racks or top of books/DVDs.

Expert level

* Move appliances, bottles, knick knacks and clean that area.

* Empty cupboards and fridge and clean inside and on top.

* Use limescale remover on sinks and bath/shower.

* Use oven cleaner on inside of oven, scrub oven shelves.

Basic household calamities

OH NO! YOU HAVE...

... SPILT RED WINE — **YES**

NO

... BURNT FOOD ONTO TRAY — **YES**

NO

... A DIRTY IRON — **YES**

NO

... BEEN SICK — **YES**

NO

... TRODDEN IN MUD — **YES**

NO

... SCUFFED WALL — **YES**

Blot/dab spill with dry kitchen roll and then cold water. Apply a little white wine and baking soda. Hoover up the soda.

Wipe dry dirt off with kitchen towel. Pour boiling water on to tray, add 1 tsp baking soda and let sit. Rinse and clean as usual.

Buff a small amount of toothpaste onto the plate and then rinse with cloth. Set iron to steam for 5 minutes.

Scoop up excess sick. Sprinkle baking soda on and let stand. Mix washing-up liquid and white vinegar with lots of warm water and sponge stain.

Let mud dry. Vacuum up mud and spritz detergent on affected area. Dab with dry kitchen roll.

Mix baking soda with warm water. Apply to wall with soft cloth and scrub gently.

ADULTING
TIMETABLE

Are you brimming with good ideas but aren't sure how you'll balance it all together? Fill out this timetable to get you started. You don't have to stick to everything but this is a good way to see what works for you and what needs to change.

	7 a.m.–9 a.m.	9 a.m.–1 p.m.	1 p.m.–1.30 p.m.	1 30 p.m.–5 p.m.	5 p.m.–5 30 p.m.	6 30 p.m.–7 p.m.	7 p.m.–8 p.m	8 p.m.–bedtime
Sun								
Sat								
Fri								
Thur								
Wed								
Tues								
Mon								

MIC DROP

Congratulations! You have completed all of adulting! We can picture you now, cleaning the floor between push-ups, a full roast cooking in the oven and your canvas and paints in the corner of the room just waiting for you to complete your masterpiece...

Oh, don't be silly! We're just like your parents – all we want for you is to be healthy, happy and the best person you can be. Hopefully you'll have found some tips in these pages that have helped you on that path. Remember that the true essence of adulting doesn't really lie in small bowls of food or nice cushions but in having enough time to do what you love as well as what you must.

Good luck on your journey; we're very proud of you!

IMAGE CREDITS

p.6 © Carboxylase/Shutterstock.com
p.12 © Happy Art/Shutterstock.com
p.17 © paradesign/Shutterstock.com
p.27 © robuart/Shutterstock.com
p.37 © venimo/Shutterstock.com
p.38 © Carboxylase/Shutterstock.com
pp.50–51 © Everilda/Shutterstock.com
p.58 © elenabsl/Shutterstock.com
p.60 © Carboxylase/Shutterstock.com
p.70 © In-Finity/Shutterstock.com
p.72 © Carboxylase/Shutterstock.com
p.90 © Carboxylase/Shutterstock.com
p.93 hand © bioraven/Shutterstock.com
p.93 chef's hat © fractalgr/Shutterstock.com
p.94 house © n o o m/Shutterstock.com
p.94 shelf © a Sk/Shutterstock.com
p.96 thermometer © GzP_Design/Shutterstock.com
p.96 whisk, measuring spoons © Mickicev Atelje/Shutterstock.com
p.96 springform cake tin © Park Ji Sun/Shutterstock.com
p.96 blender © Serhiy Smirnov/Shutterstock.com
p.96 tongs © fractalgr/Shutterstock.com
p.96 dish © Hein Nouwens/Shutterstock.com
p.96 pizza cutter, ladle, potato masher © Hein Nouwens/Shutterstock.com
p.96 juicer © Yustus/Shutterstock.com
p.96 steamer © davooda/Shutterstock.com
p.100 flowers © Svetlana_Okeana/Shutterstock.com
p.100 sun © Sergei Boshkirov/Shutterstock.com
p.101 leaf © Natasha Pankina/Shutterstock.com
p.101 snowflake © Hein Nouwens/Shutterstock.com
p.102 © Z-art/Shutterstock.com
p.109 © browndogstudios/Shutterstock.com
p.114 © Carboxylase/Shutterstock.com
p.118 © IhorZigor/Shutterstock.com
p.121 © browndogstudios/Shutterstock.com
p.124 © Carboxylase/Shutterstock.com

Piggy bank on pp.1, 5–7, 9–97, 99–115, 117–126, 128
© Titov Nikola/Shutterstock.com

If you're interested in finding out more about our books, find us on Facebook at **SUMMERSDALE PUBLISHERS** and follow us on Twitter at **@SUMMERSDALE**.

WWW.SUMMERSDALE.COM